USGov.fix

FIXES FOR A FAILING GOVERNMENT

Tom Hopper

Revised Edition: USGov.Fix (2010)
Copyright © 2011 Tom Hopper
All Rights Reserved

ISBN: 1453757600
ISBN-13: 9781453757604

ACKNOWLEDGEMENTS

*Too my wife Marilyn, my Daughter
Karen and her husband Lew Buckley*

TABLE OF CONTENTS
USGOV.FIX (3rd Edition)

Fix Strategy

The Institutional Fixes

Final Recapitulation and Strategy

INTRODUCTION
The Author and USCGOV.FIX

Tom Brokaw called us, the soldiers of WWII, "The Greatest Generation." While I appreciate the accolade, I think the greatest generations were those of our forefathers. They brought this country to its finest hours. We were the children of their greatness, and we served because it was expected of us.

The 1940's were certainly among the greatest years in the history of the United States; every citizen, whether serviceman/woman or civilian, worked as one, creating the greatest synergy of all time to save the world from collapse. In the process, they created a national community fiber never before achieved.

I grew up in the Great Depression. A 1938 high school graduate with no prospect of attending college, I started as a factory worker. In 1943, service called, and I eventually shipped out for the European front where I served in the field artillery until the end of the War. After returning home, I was fortunate to pioneer in computers and communications, both here and abroad. Among other things, I had the opportunity to work with the US Chamber of

Commerce in developing systems to improve international trade, and I was invited to speak at the World Trade Center in that capacity. Following retirement, I served two terms as a county legislator in my home state of New York.

During my lifetime, I saw the rise and fall of dictatorships, and the collapse of the French and British empires. I am very concerned about the degree of commonality I see between current circumstances in the US and the conditions that led to those collapses. It is disturbing to look back to the end of WWII, when we thought we had made the world safe for our children, only to find our country in the perilous conditions of today.

I have been a student of history and government for 75 years. I always had great faith in our government, and I have always believed (and still do) that the crafting of Constitution was the most significant event in our history. My one concern was the country's wild economic swings. I thought in the mid-1990's that the government finally had the economy under control; but then came 2008, which completely destroyed that image.

After the Iraq debacle and the 2008 financial meltdown, I decided to do a detailed analysis to determine the causes of such a massive failure of government and to propose the changes that need to be made to effect repairs. This book is the result of that analysis.

CHAPTER 1

Why USGOV.FIX

USGOV is the URL prefix for access to the government; FIX means repairing things that are broken. The government is broken and needs to be fixed.

At this writing (Dec 2011), the 2012 election process is already well under way, with the usual carnival atmosphere. I can only hide my head in shame as I think of my WWII buddies in European graves who gave their lives to sustain this mockery.

So let's get to work.

In 1776 the United States was established with a new Constitution, beginning with the following Preamble:

"We the people of the United States, in Order to form a more perfect Union, establish Justice, insure domestic Tranquility, provide for the common defence, promote the general Welfare, and secure the Blessings of Liberty to ourselves and our Posterity, do ordain and establish this Constitution for the United States of America."

We will start with a challenge to citizens!

The United States of America has resources adequate to meet every need; land to provide our food, resources needed to clothe and shelter our people, the best technical resources in the world, a dedicated work force, and a homogenous population that gives unwavering support to its leaders. In short, we have all the elements needed to create the perfect Union referred to in the Preamble.

Why then do we have massive unemployment, social services bringing us close to bankruptcy, loss of faith in leadership, a failing education system, industry fleeing to other countries, and a growing poverty level in which children are poorly fed? The list goes on and on.

The answer, to put it bluntly, is a failing system. That's right, a failing system; there is no other answer!

Is it systemic design or human failure that has brought us to this point? To evaluate why the system is failing is the purpose of USGOV.FIX. The time is critical--the 2012 elections could well be a historical turning point in the survival of the nation envisioned by the founders.

CHAPTER 2
The Shock

An avid student of government, I spent my working years in industry using Information Technology (IT) in support of international trade; I spoke at the World Trade Center in that regard. After retiring, I served two terms as a County Legislator in New York State. I lived through and saw the constant erosion of our great nation, and like many citizens I had faith that things would be fixed. Then came 2008, when the financial community savaged the nation with the worst abuse of power in history, causing the greatest recession since the 1930's and nearly bankrupting the country.

I was dumb-shocked; how could this happen? What was happening to our country? Why a recession, why unemployment, why a no-win war, why loss of faith in government, why a crisis in health-care, why a falling dollar, why, why, why? I had to find the answers.

As a pioneer in (IT), my approach was and remains analytical. It started with a review of the Constitution. I found it to be a practical vision in institutional logic, as well as a model appropriate to today's systemic theory. The Constitutional model defined the rules to be followed (legislature/laws), an organization for execution (chief executive), a feedback

mechanism (State of the Union Address), and an audit function to monitor the integrity of the model (Judiciary).

The next step was to determine the adequacy of the Constitution to manage a government. There was no question
that its broad framework had to be expanded to provide a
detailed set of laws to manage the nation. Future leaders
were given the responsibility for this task.

I then searched history for an overview of the nation to
date. I was disappointed to find little; there were no top-
down looks at the overall development of the country. I
found my 70 years of study and 30 years of involvement
with government were invaluable.

USGOV.FIX will review the country's development from its
beginning, search for the causes of our current condition,
and recommend fixes. The intent is to energize citizens to
initiate a constructive movement, using the new electronic
media to fix the failures. If Libya can be liberated with Twitter we can use the same media to get the Nation back on
track.

CHAPTER 3
Setting the Stage

To most citizens, their image of the Constitution is based on the elegant wordage in the Preamble. The Constitution itself is the legal institutional foundation of our government, establishing its rules; and it is the derivation of the laws we live by today. The Constitution was the legal framework for a Federal Constitutional Republic, its laws and liberties, the structure of government and rules for leadership selection.

The book is a systemic evaluation of government. It will deal with both the institutional as well as the social (or so-called socio-economic) structure. We will avoid extensive use of systemic language; however, there is a lot of smokescreen around the whole governmental process, so let's establish a mutual understanding of the most significant terms.

Citizens have been led to believe the political system and the government are the same. This is one of the major perceptual flaws; politics are the citizens' interface to government, whose supposed purpose is to provide quality leadership.

The terms "institution" or "institutional" will be used to identify the combined governmental branches, Legislative, Executive and Judiciary. The term "Executive" will identify the executive branch. The term "Congress" will identify the House and Senate. The House and Senate will be explicit definitions.

Laws are the legal establishment of rules! We will use the terms "rules" and "laws" throughout the book, but to the reader they are implicitly the same.

We will use the term "Nation" to identify the United States of America. We will use the term "community" to identify all citizens of the nation. Terms for specific segments such as "legal community" might be used. The term "population" will be used to identify all persons, both citizens and non-citizens, living within the geographic and legal control of the nation.

We will use the term "State-of-the-State" to identify the condition of the nation at any given point. "States" will mean the combined States of the nation.

On a systemic note, "infrastructure" is the basic structure of a system. It may be used at various levels: ie: there is an "economic infrastructure" within the overall "governmental infrastructure". A good infrastructure is systemically and logically designed. All systems have an infrastructure, but empirically some "just growed".

The term "control" will be used often and requires a warning: Control means keeping a system within defined limits.

There have been and are community members who have used their great freedom to rail against any form of government inhibition. They espouse the word "control" to portray an image of mind control by an insidious government. Control is a good word and a critical factor in any system. Without control there is chaos!

On a personal note, I use the term "renegade" to identify community and population members who put personal agenda ahead of their nation. I also use the terms "hysteria" and "smokescreen" to identify political hype used to blind citizens as to the real state of affairs. These terms are not intended to be offensive, only the most representative possible.

Systemically, we will be using the terms "variables" and "disturbances". Variables are the factors that must be regulated (controlled) to have an effective system. Disturbances are factors that are unable or difficult to control and can cause a system to fail. Don't get hung up on these, their use will be obvious.

Finally, this study is a "top down" analysis of government. The evaluations made are broad and are based on obvious historical conclusions. Complete books could be written on any of the subjects involved, but the breadth of the subject precludes over-involvement in detail.

CHAPTER 4

The Visionary Challenge

What did the designers face in establishing a new nation? Civilization has seen every conceivable type of government, from dictator to democracy.

In theory, any type of governmental system can be created and function; the measure of success is the quality of its systemic base. Communism in Russia was a woeful effort in that regard. It also failed in China, which has since converted to a capitalistic oligarchy while maintaining an ostensibly communist façade. Socialism has been successful to a limited degree, most notably in Scandinavia. Europe has several parliamentary nations with substantial social support that are struggling financially. Nations like Greece have virtually bankrupted themselves with excessive social programs. Emerging nations are struggling to establish effective governments, but most are hampered by centuries of ethnic insularity, religious dogma and corruption.

There have been no ironclad examples of perfect government, and there will probably not be in the lifetime of even the youngest of our readers. Freedom, which implied democracy, was the major concern for the new nation; however, democracy in pure form relegates the minority to second-class status. The result of the founders' effort to protect the rights of all citizens was a Constitutional Democratic Republic. It was to be a representative government with leaders selected by its citizens.

The result of the founders' vision was the United States of America. In a little over two centuries, this embryonic nation created the greatest wealth and power in history.

This study will examine both the institutional (government) and undefined (socio-economic) infrastructures, as well as the growth factors leading to the state-of-the-state in 2012.

CHAPTER 5

The Constitution

The United States of America as a nation is one of the most unusual in the history of civilization. Blessed with boundless natural resources, its founders cleared the land and built a nation of freedom, wealth and privilege that no country has ever known.

In 1776 a small group of men established its Constitution, which still stands. This magnificent document provided the legal framework for a Federal Constitutional Republic and defined the governmental structure.

Three bodies were assigned to run the government.

The Legislature was to be the primary governmental functionary, making laws and managing the finances. It was called Congress and consisted of two bodies (bicameral), the House of Representatives and the Senate.

The Executive function was to manage the day-to-day operations of government under the laws created by the Legislature.

The Judiciary function, headed by a Supreme Court, was to handle legalities.

Legislators and the Chief Executive were to be elected officials. Judiciary officials were to be appointed by the Executive branch, subject to approval by the Senate.

The Constitution was a legal framework for a representative government. It identified the governmental structure, law making and enforcement. It identified several liberties, the right to bear arms and others. It identified timing and rules for elections and succession when needed. A major objective was to establish a balance of power and negate any possibility of a monarchy. The Constitution was and remains a legal framework for a Democratic Republic, the United States of America.

Volumes have been written about the visionaries and their roles in developing the Constitution. It involved the usual wheeling and dealing concomitant with any organizational development. The nation's population was roughly 2.5 million, about the same as Chicago today. It was primarily a frontier community consisting of a few colonies and states. Few of today's relevant factors, such as social needs and the economy were even mentioned. A monumental effort and decades of development would be required before a stable institutional infrastructure could be established.

If not having done so recently, the reader should take a break and read/review the US Constitution. It is further suggested that readers might also review the constitutions of other countries, which are most enlightening. All are available on the Internet.

Following this brief introduction to the nation's founding will be a summary of its growth.

CHAPTER 6

1776 - 1952: The Initial Years

The initial years were filled with growing pains; freedom was a mandate for exploitation. A few people became very rich, and Wall Street had more wealth and power than Washington, an unfortunate corollary to the condition today.

The early years were filled with abuses, from stealing the land from Native Americans to slavery. Exploitation was rampant; pristine streams were polluted with industrial and human waste, forests denuded, buffalo slaughtered almost to extinction, rich farming soils exploited and reduced to sand. The land was laid waste. Labor was abused, with twelve-hour work days six and seven days a week. Coal miners worked in horrible conditions, with a sacrificial canary their only safety warning.

Government could not get its act together. The primary institutional power assigned to the Legislature was defaulted to the Executive branch, which has been dominant to this day. Governing was a constant turf battle between the legislative and executive branches, strategic decisions were short term, and the constitutional vision was ignored. The establishment of the government defined in the Constitution was defaulted to a rambling empirical process leading to the fragile infrastructure of today. This fragility was exacerbated as political parties developed, infiltrating and eventually dominating governmental operations.

The transfer of power to the executive branch might have been less significant if adequate leaders could have been selected. Executive leadership has been inadequate almost from the beginning. An early President closed down the national bank. Following were a string of inadequate leaders who could not hold the nation together. Slavery was a major factor leading to secession by slave states and the resulting Civil War. It was the most tragic time in the country's history, with 600,000 young citizens killed to ostensibly free a million slaves. The result was a hundred years of humiliation and poverty before blacks were given equal treatment, the scars of which have never been completely erased.

The country moved from the original frontier to an agrarian society, and farming communities developed their own infrastructures, including banks. This decentralized and stabilized to some degree the nation's finances.

A major change occurred in the late 1800's and early 1900's, when the country entered the industrial age. Through exploitation and ingenuity, the community built great wealth, converting resources such as iron ore to metals, cotton to cloth, and building industrial empires, the principal one being automobiles. This unfettered industrial juggernaut created the greatest wealth ever achieved and a nation that could not fail. However, the economic infrastructure "just growed" empirically, and with industrial success, money moved back to Wall Street.

Government initially ignored exploitation but finally took action when it was obvious that unhealthy capitalistic practices were developing. Government was both a help and a hindrance. There was a constant battle between the central government, the industrial community, and the states to clean up restrictions and establish a free and open economy.

The growth years were a "boom or bust" economic roller coaster ride, with 47 documented recessions finally resulting in the great depression of the 1930's, when economic conditions were worse than in 2008. Bank failures were common, one fourth of workers were unemployed, and there was almost a complete breakdown. The catastrophic condition resulted in massive government investments in the economic infrastructure, again a corollary to the 2008 recession. The first governmental stabilizing factors were initiated, including guarantees of bank deposits and creation of the Security and Exchange Commission and the Social Security system. These have provided some benefit but have not provided the necessary security and stability.

During this period, a rise in unionism brought shorter work weeks; benefits such as pension and healthcare were instituted; and safety measures were enacted improving working conditions, particularly for coal miners.

The country rebounded after the great depression with the greatest industrial effort in history, producing the armaments and the manpower necessary to defeat fascism in Europe and a senseless war initiated by Japan.

The great depression was turned around, WWII was successfully completed, a third world war in Asia was avoided, and a common frontier in Europe was established that curtailed centuries of bickering and distrust. The nation in 1952 was a healthy and dynamic industrial force with relatively few problems.

In retrospect, the heroic community effort of the 1940's may have saved the nation. The democratic republic was close to collapse in the great depression, and there is no way of knowing what type of government would have resulted had this happened.

The initial years were a rambling and uncoordinated phenomenon, perhaps what might be expected of a new nation. While the country grew empirically, the vision of the democratic republic was ignored.

CHAPTER 7

1952 - 2008: The Turbulent Years

By 1952 the US had reached its zenith in power, continuing to increase its wealth. As savings and wealth grew, Wall Street consolidated its financial dominance over the nation.

The turbulent years comprised a period of historic and devastating events, from putting a man on the moon to a senseless war in Vietnam, killing 58,000 of our young men. During this period, the nation saw the ultimate inadequacy of the political system, when for the first time a presidency was bought. We recognized that dependence on foreign oil was a strategic blunder but allowed the creation of the most debilitating energy monopoly ever. We allowed the transfer of our wealth-creating industrial might to other countries. We ignored the problem of immigration and its implication to future population growth and ethnic distribution. We allowed the failure of our educational system to keep up with other nations. And we ignored the transfer of wealth to Wall Street and allowed the transfer of governmental power to the financial community. The list is endless.

The turbulent years were also a period of abject governmental failure. It was a period of instant gratification initiated by a liberal Supreme Court. All sense of responsibility was lost, criminals were coddled, disciplinary spanking became child abuse, money was easy, and spending exceeded income. The 1960's saw the beginnings of social reforms leading to the tentative financial state of today. By 1980 the country was out of control, with dependence on foreign oil and loss of wealth-creating industries taking their toll. The national debt, which had been steadily declining since WWII, became to climb again as astronomical government spending and voodoo economics took over.

Economists convinced industry that it was better to send our wealth-creating industries overseas and buy the cheaper products they would return. We built strip malls and subsidized their growth, eventually becoming their debtors. What was left of the industrial community lost its way, management failed in every sense, from cost control to product quality, market needs, and long term planning. Short-term goals based on immediate profit and blind vision to the world's changing needs was the norm. Excessive labor costs brought about by years of management concessions were the final blow. Lawlessness was rampant, investors were lied to, and cooking the books was the norm as major corporations fell by the wayside. The unfettered juggernaut that had created the greatest wealth in history was decimated.

The wealth-creating labor force was also decimated, with white collar workers increasing from thirty to sixty percent of the work force. Two million people were employed in government at a cost of one and a half trillion dollars per year. The private sector went from a self-sufficient wealth-creating industrial base to a service economy, as costs spiraled out of control.

Financial management mirrored and exploited the industrial failure. Short-term goals and executive perks were the primary objective. There was a feeding frenzy as the wealth accumulated by Wall Street was used to buy up failing industries, strip off and sell the healthy portions for a quick profit, and scrap the rest. Wall Street consolidated its wealth and created financial empires "too big to fail".

There was a brief respite at the end of the century when the economy turned around. This was quickly negated in the new century by a politically motivated tax reduction and a senseless attack on a theocracy that was no threat, bringing another no-win war killing 5000 of our brave young men and women and maiming thousands more. This catastrophic blunder, one of the most devastating in the country's history, exacerbated a terrorism threat that could cause the deaths of our children for generations and might well be the precursor to another world conflict.

Government did nothing to stem the flow as the country spun out of control, even exacerbating the problem by borrowing money to maintain a life style beyond its means. There had to be a crash and there was! The wealth that citizens had turned over to Wall Street was squandered. Creative methods were developed to expand risky lending practices and skim off trillions of dollars, destroying the pensions of millions of citizens and putting the country close to bankruptcy.

It was the most deplorable community abuse in history.

It left us in 2008 with a country in its worst fiscal condition since the great depression, wallowing in debt, with nothing in sight to get us back on track. We were in a no-win war thousands of miles from home. We had lost face in the world community, and our once invincible dollar was being devalued every day. High unemployment and loss of faith in government took their toll.

How could this great country be riding the crest and fall so deeply in a few short years? Did government fail to see or simply ignore the oncoming crisis, or is the system so flawed that there was no fix? There were flaws that could have been fixed but were not, but the greatest cause was the failure of the political process to provide quality leadership.

Chapter 8

State-of-the-State Recapitulation – 2012

Let's pause for a moment to review.

I tried to be as positive as possible in the growth of the nation, but it had to be a realistic scenario. The major portion of my life was spent in the turbulent years of which I was an active participant. My description of those years was gleaned from active participation as well as coverage by newspapers, magazine and television.

I was involved in national activities through participation in technical societies. I worked with the US Commerce Department and international organizations in developing standards to improve trade, and I spoke at the World Trade Center in that regard. I worked extensively with IBM, AT&T and other industrial and technical companies and was extremely fortunate to be in the vanguard of computer and communications technology. I was at the forefront of Information Technology through those years, and I feel my review of the nation's growth was accurately defined. I hope the reader agrees.

What did we learn from the review? As any new organization or society develops, growing pains are normal.

Developing a new nation certainly expands those by a substantial magnitude.

My major observation and concern was the quality of leadership. After the original visionaries, there should have been a few disciples who could sustain the momentum.

The legislative default to the executive branch was certainly a telling blow, aborting the structure of government. Growth then became a rambling, uncoordinated effort spread among a wide variety of leaders. Commitment to the Constitution varied by individual leader, a phenomenon that seems to continue to this day. Why have we not been able to create statesman who could lead the nation to the constitutional vision?

This of course points out the complete inadequacy of the political process, which, as we face the 2012 election, is continuing the same carnival atmosphere in producing new candidates.

We will next move on to a more detailed analysis of the growth of the nation.

CHAPTER 9
Congress: The Institutional View

The Constitution, in Article I Section I, says of the Legislative Branch: "All Legislative powers herein granted shall be vested in a Congress of the United States, which shall consist of a Senate and House of Representatives." Section 5, Paragraph 2, says: "Each House may determine the Rules of its Proceedings, punish its Members for disorderly Behavior, and, with the Concurrence of two-thirds, expel a Member."

The Constitution gave Congress primary governmental power to write the laws by which the Constitutional Republic could be created and managed. It was given free reign, even to creating its own rules and procedures. It was assigned control of the finances, revenue, commerce, raising armies and most other governmental responsibilities. Congress was to be the base, the bedrock for the creation of the perfect Union described in the Preamble.

The key to the Congressional role is its Constitutional power to create its own rules and procedures. In any new organization given complete authority to write its own rules of procedure, the usual practice is for its members to take care of themselves first. Congress did that very well!

The procedures they developed and still follow are an incongruous hodge-podge of rules. They were designed (rather defaulted) to maintain complete authority of the current power group, regardless of the impact on the nation. With no seniority restrictions, they could build dynasties that could endure forever. This was fertile ground for political parties to infiltrate and eventually control government.

This country probably would have survived those shortcomings if Congress had ever fulfilled its Constitutional role. Instead, it defaulted its institutional role to the Executive branch, creating a fragmented governmental infrastructure that continues to this day. Congress never filled its role, and that was unquestionably the greatest failure in implementing the Constitution. The implications are still being felt today; indicative of its continued failure is their 2011 confidence rating by citizens of roughly 9%. I tried to determine if there were significant factors leading to, or responsible for, the congressional failure but could not. Early on, the executive branch assumed primary governmental control; and a confrontational role with the legislative branch seems to have been in effect almost from the beginning.

In hindsight, the job of creating the rules for the new country was as staggering as executive leadership. Were the needs to lead so great and the support of Congress so ineffective that the transfer of power was necessary? Perhaps there are historians who can answer the question.

A major question regarding Congress is the structure itself: Are two houses necessary? The Senate seems to have more power than its representation suggests. Was the bicameral decision an additional Constitutional ploy to limit the balance of power? Has the existences of two houses perhaps avoided some derelict executive decisions? The terrible decisions of the past 50 years lend no credence to that supposition.

Congress has allowed Government lawmaking to be taken over by a lobbyist community that spends over three billion dollars a year influencing lawmaking for the benefit of its sponsors. The result is hastily and poorly written laws (many by lobbyists) that result in a swollen and ineffective legal community and exorbitant court costs. A prime example is the 2009 healthcare bill, which is already being challenged.

Lobbyists can also provide election campaign funds not only to Congress but to any other institutional branch of government; and recent Supreme Court decisions support this shameful condition.

Congress' failure in lawmaking is probably exceeded by its poor financial oversight. The 2008 financial disaster was brought about by years of political pandering to the financial community through vehicles such as Fannie Mae and Freddie Mac. This was exacerbated by a political decision to lessen financing requirements for housing. The resulting housing boom created the opportunity for the financial community's 2008 abuse. Congress saw the impending debacle but delayed taking action, hoping it would just go away. To have oversight responsibility for the country's finances in the hands of incompetent congressional committees challenges all reason.

Perhaps the greatest fault of Congress is its infiltration and dominance by the political system. Congress has become an ingrained political hierarchy that dominates all governmental functions. Legislative leaders have (political) life and death control over their members. New legislators arriving in Washington are herded into ideological pens that place party ahead of the nation.

This has created an atmosphere in which political infighting and bashing have become so bitter that reconciliation is out of the question. There is no across-the-aisle dialogue as to what is best for the country; only what is best for the party is considered. Governmental lawmaking is controlled by the political party in power in ways that are often directly opposed to the good of the people.

Congress is the most undemocratic organization in a democratic society. Its ability to pigeonhole good legislation and add earmarks to new legislation, costing taxpayers billions of dollars, adds to the nausea. For a country that has developed with limited corruption, Congressional earmarks are the major remaining stigma.

A shameful exposition is the endless string of TV hearings seemingly designed for political posturing rather than for addressing the nation's myriad problems.

Seniority has failed in virtually every organization ever established, and Congress is no exception.

To add to their failings, insider trading by legislators has recently come to light.

A final caveat: There are no term limits for congress. Under their seniority rules, poor performers with constituency backing can continue in office forever. The Speaker of the House can potentially become the most powerful person in the world simply by continuing to be elected.

It is troubling to make such damning criticism of the major branch of government, but this perception of their inadequacy is reinforced by community evaluation. One can only wonder why this deplorable condition has been allowed to continue, the only logical answer is citizen malaise.

CHAPTER 10

The Executive Branch

Article II (the Executive Branch) Section 1 states, "The executive power shall be vested in a President of the United States of America."

The Constitution gave the Chief Executive responsibility for day-to-day governmental operations, under rules and procedures (laws) established by the legislature. With Congress' dereliction of responsibility, the Chief Executive assumed the primary role, making policy as well as managing day-to-day operations. This created a vacuum that allowed a takeover by the political process, again resulting in the fragmented and ineffective government of today.

While a monarchial takeover has been avoided, the Constitutional objective of an executive running day-to-day governmental operations under laws created by the legislature has escalated to a world leader with more power than any monarch in the history of civilization. This might have had a positive effect if the political system had provided statesman who could have been world leaders and still have governed effectively. Instead, they provided inadequate candidates who would prostrate themselves to party politics. The result: a rambling, uncoordinated government and constantly shifting political focus with little perception of need. The vital signs of stagnation were ignored.

This increase in executive power has had drastic consequences. The results of executive dereliction in the last fifty years have included senseless and destructive wars, crushing debt, financial instability, loss of faith in government, and loss of citizen representation. The list goes on and on.

The causal relationship of executive power to the operation of the country is extreme. Presidential elections have become so volatile that they create a degree of disturbance that shakes the entire institutional and economic infrastructure. They are the country's most destabilizing force, and their inadequacy has become a joke and a disaster. To win elections, the political system is taken over by deep pockets that pour money into a few critical states, disenfranchising a large portion of citizens.

Political payback exacerbates the destabilizing election impact and causes major disturbances. Post-election shuffling creates vicious cycles that reverberate across the entire governmental and community base.

In summary, the increase in the power of the chief executive has created a pseudo- monarchial phenomenon that creates disturbing cycles across the US and the global universe. This power source goes far beyond the needs of a civilized country of 300 million people. It is destabilizing to government and its citizens, and it is disruptive to the building of a strong nation.

CHAPTER 11
The Judicial Process

There is a phenomenon in most professions whereby the developers create a unique language to insulate their particular methodology. I observed this as a pioneer in the computer field. As the world's second oldest profession, the legal community is a glaring example; citizens are dependent on the whereas and wherefores in all matters of law.

The Constitution created a Supreme Court to establish and maintain the Judicial function. It was given a more explicit institutional role than the Legislative and Executive branches. It was to be the arbiter of the legal process and the adjudicator of constitutional law, the legal framework for a democratic republic. Congress' law-making inadequacy has created a vacuum, resulting in the Supreme Court's having become the country's default lawmaker. Since its inception, the legal community has dominated the institutional government, showing no interest in giving up that role.

The Judiciary has done nothing to improve the effectiveness of their profession. One of the most significant failures is the court system, which has an impact on cost escalation in every aspect of community affairs. Every dollar of cost in healthcare carries the burden of excessive insurance for medical claims and their ridiculous awards. Healthcare, however, is only one example of the detrimental impact of frivolous and excessive court awards; there are countless others. The judiciary makes no effort to contain this practice, allowing it to continue unabated. In testimony to this are telephone yellow pages and TV ads claiming seven figure awards for everything from birth defects to whatever. It is a shameful exposition.

A major failing is to provide a more precise and understandable legal language. The inability of a legal language to reach closure results in hung juries, continued litigation, and unnecessary costs to litigants. As a result, the legal costs to the community are disastrous. Estimated costs for legal services approach a trillion dollars per year, or $5000 per family.

In summary, it is disconcerting to see the honorable constitutional judicial role denigrated to the low status it to which it has fallen. We have a professional, judicial role that should attract the brightest of our people, being performed at a level totally inadequate for this great country.

CHAPTER 12

Government Structure and Organization

The Constitution was and remains a valid systemic vision for a democratic republic. A balance of power was a basic requirement, and the separation of the legislative and executive branches would have met that need.

The failure by Congress to assume its constitutional role changed the structure of government completely.

The primary governmental power assumed by the Executive Branch takes the form of a flat organizational structure that may have been adequate in 1786 but does not meet the needs of today. In the Executive Branch, the Chief Executive must manage (in addition to the Vice President) 12 office organizations, 15 cabinet level departments and roughly 56 independent establishments and government corporations. To have direct responsibility over 80 plus functions is completely unworkable and has undoubtedly been a factor in executive ineffectiveness.

This structural and organizational weakness does not provide the level of effectiveness necessary to manage a huge governmental complex. It also causes major disturbances when there is a political change in the chief executive;

the entire government is shaken up as political payback appointees replace current managers. Vicious cycles are the result, and these reverberate across the entire government.

Structure and organization are major factors in governmental effectiveness. With a competent staff, decisions can be made at the appropriate level or, if necessary, expedited quickly to the next level. Qualified managers can be effective and committed. With a poor organizational structure, good managers are going to be frustrated and leave. Poor managers will continue in office, live with the frustration, and wait for the pension, all the result a bloated bureaucracy.

The causal effect of a fragmented government structure also creates a critical weakness in representation. The State of the Union address, originally meant to provide a community interface, has become an inadequate political placebo. The three quarters Congressional/State requirement for referendums virtually negates a citizen interface. The limited number of Constitutional amendments in 225 years is adequate testimony to this evaluation.

CHAPTER 13
The Political Process

The political system is one of representative government's greatest needs and gravest threats. *Its greatest need* is to provide capable leaders to manage the government. *Its gravest threat* is that the political system infiltrates and controls government operations.

US citizens lose on both counts!

The founders were concerned with the potential rise of political parties, and their vision was justified. The two political parties that have arisen are based on divergent philosophies.

On the positive side, divergent views are normal phenomena in any organization; and for government it does provide some balance. Divergent views may have been effective in maintaining our fragmented government, as we have not yet tripped over the line to monarchy or socialism.

On the negative side, the divergence in ideology has become a political ploy destroying all sense of reality. It has created an atmosphere so destructive that it has brought government to its knees. The recent fiasco regarding the national debt crisis and the failure of the "Super Committee" to create a debt reduction plan is credible evidence for this evaluation.

A major ploy used by the political system for control over citizens is hysteria over taxes. Today the term "taxation" is an anathema, a word that no politician dares to utter and one that leads with certainty to a lost election. Taxes have become an anathema because the public has seen the abuses, the waste, the earmarks, and other failings brought about by politicians ineffectiveness. One hundred years ago, the community appreciated the country they lived in and met their responsibility, be it paying taxes or serving in the armed forces. We can either make our country strong again by going back to doing our share, or continue the downward spiral.

The result of political inadequacy is lost citizens' representation, the most crucial part of our democratic republic. Elections have been taken over by political parties with deep pockets. It's not outright buying of votes, but the result is the same; presidential elections are a mockery and a farce.

We endure the political posturing, the endless and worthless debates, and millions of dollars spent shuttling people all over the country to stamp out the latest soft spot in the never-ending polls. These are followed by endless speeches of froth with no substance, and personal attacks that have no place in any conversation, much less in the election of one of the world's leaders. Presidential elections are a sham and a shame, an affront to every citizen, and a humiliating exhibition before the rest of the world. The forthcoming 2012 election promises to be the epitome of political sleaze.

The political system is one of the nation's most destructive forces, one that, if not fixed, may well lead to the end of the democratic republic.

CHAPTER 14

The Community

Citizens, the most important part of the governmental equation and the most ignored, have become nameless statistics within a fragmented government.

There is an anomaly here that challenges all logic. Citizens have been the victims of government's failure: their children have been killed and maimed through outrageous military actions; they have become disenfranchised in voting by the electoral process; the judiciary has failed to protect them from ridiculous and pernicious lawsuits; the financial community has been allowed to destroy their savings; and they are subjected to smokescreen and hysteria in the political process. The ultimate failure has been their loss of citizen rights and representation, the implicit foundation of the Constitutional Republic envisioned in the Constitution.

In spite of these abuses, this nation has the most dedicated citizens in the world. This Constitutional Republic created a hegemony that has never been seen before and will probably never be seen again. Citizens still have faith that the current problems can be overcome and that we can return to the lifestyle existent following the victory in WWII.

Citizens will again be the major factor in overcoming the mistakes of the past and building a new and bright future. But time is critical; there is a limit to the patience of even the most dedicated.

Street riots, no matter how civil, cannot be ignored.

CHAPTER 15

Recapitulation – Government's Institutional Performance

We find a fragmented government, the result of inadequate leadership. There were no leaders who could or would shape the democratic republic defined in the Constitution, so the country's development defaulted to an empirical process that is skewed towards legalities with a lack of emphasis on socio-economic requirements. This led to a fragmented infrastructure and a tentative economic base.

Congress' paramount failure was defaulting their primary Constitutional assignment. The assumption by the Executive Branch of the primary power resulted in turf issues that continue to this time. This was exacerbated by Congress's further default to the political process. The result has been an institutional Government growing empirically, meandering from crisis to crisis with no commitment to building a stable and lasting infrastructure.

Our government is poorly structured, organized, and managed as a result of being infiltrated and dominated by political parties. It is a government so permeated by politics that there is no reasonable dialogue between the parties representing the people. This constantly-shifting power base has floundered, making bad decisions that have put our country into a downward spiral for the last 50 years.

Constitutional concern for the balance of power has been ignored, and there have been disastrous consequences of executive actions taken with the support of weak legislatures. Prime examples are the senseless wars in Viet Nam and Iraq that killed tens of thousands of our children.

Institutional failure has resulted in a government virtually controlled by the 17,000 lobbyists who pour 3.5 billion dollars each year into influence peddling.

Their activities include actually writing laws, making huge campaign contributions, and any or all other tasks required to support a renegade community. Recent decisions by the Supreme Court support this deplorable condition.

On the socio-economic side, government failure in the institutional elements was only exceeded by its inability to address the social needs of the community. All social services are in trouble, and there is a crisis in healthcare.

On the spending side, government has failed to manage the country's finances. Tough decisions on taxation and funding have been swept under the rug. The political establishment in control of government will not face these issues; instead, like immature children, they have borrowed to fill budgetary gaps, turning the US into a debtor nation.

Government has never been able to cope with the tentative economic infrastructure, which has gone through boom and bust cycles from the beginning. This anomaly resulted in the creation of the greatest wealth in history, but it brought the country close to bankruptcy in 2008.

So what has caused our current perilous condition? The answer, of course, is lack of leadership. The Constitution was a legal framework upon which the country could build a governmental infrastructure. The designers could not possibly define the explicit rules of day-to-day operations, so these were left to future leaders. However, instead of developing a solid infrastructure, our leaders built a rambling bureaucracy.

There are disturbing questions about the country's development. Is it conceivable that citizen malaise and political paranoia have allowed the Constitution to be used as a tool to *impede* progress? Has paranoia regarding constitutionality resulted in dogmatic reliance on the Supreme Court for lawmaking? Whatever the reason, we have an institutional system in which the tail is wagging the dog. Legalities are a critical requirement—without them there is anarchy—but they are only part of the equation needed to create a democratic republic.

The country was moved to the world forefront by its unfettered economic juggernaut that created so much wealth that the country could not fail. Unfortunately, institutional weakness derailed, abandoned, or subverted the economy, which can no longer support the social requirements imposed by inadequate leadership.

What then is the overall assessment of the State-of-the-State today? How could a country fail with so much going for it? As a nation with unlimited natural resources, no constraints, no monarch, and complete freedom, why could we not build the democratic republic the Constitution defined?

Our forefathers, through sheer will and determination, created the greatest country in the history of the world. Along the way we lost our commitment, wasted our resources, lived off the fat of the land, abandoned the principles on which the country was founded, and turned our strength and power over to others. The Constitutional vision was ignored.

It is disturbing to create such a negative appraisal of our governmental institutions. I hope that 2012 will *not* be the point that future historians identify as the beginning of the United States' regression to the status of just another third world nation.

CHAPTER 16

The Economy

The Constitution provided a basic institutional infrastructure, but the frontier community could not provide an economic infrastructure, so the economy "just growed". What "growed" was an extremely dynamic economy, the largest in the world. What should be the economic infrastructure is and always has been an unfettered, free-wheeling juggernaut.

The major components of the economy are industry and finance. With unlimited resources and a free and open society, the US industrial community created the greatest wealth in the history of the world. Industry reached its peak in the 1940's in an unprecedented outpouring of armaments necessary to winning WWII.

In the years following WWII, industry lost its way. A confrontational relationship between industry and labor resulted in the growth of unions following the great depression. In a soaring economy, unhealthy labor concessions were made, and industry fled to other countries to avoid excessive labor costs at home. American jobs were lost, and the result was the conversion of our wealth-creating industrial base to a service economy.

There was also a significant change in management philosophy. Scientific Management, initiated by the business schools, was to change the rules that industry had long observed. Sophisticated financial tools were implemented, foreshadowing the empowerment of the financial community over the economy. CEO's managerial criteria changed; the company's performance on the stock exchange became primary. Financial goals became the objective, and industrial know-how became secondary. Short-term gains were primary, and long term factors were ignored. It was the final step in the financial community's objective to become the nation's power source. Wall Street power was the precursor to the 2008 meltdown.

Economic malaise was also exacerbated by outright management failures. I worked closely with IBM in the early years of computer development. Their market strategy was to use their lead in IT development to control the computer market. They failed completely, lost billions of dollars, lost tens of thousands of jobs, defaulted their technical expertise to Microsoft, and finally faded into the consulting froth.

The auto industry was an even more pathetic example, building inefficient cars in the face of an oil crisis.

Industrial malaise was a frightful thing to observe. There was a feeding frenzy for the financial sector, which purchased what healthy firms were left, tore them apart, sold off the healthy portions for a quick profit, and closed the rest. The industrial community was decimated.

Government defaulted its responsibility by allowing unhealthy mergers and acquisitions. In the 45 years from 1930 to 1975 there were 19; in the 32 years from 1975 to 2007 that number jumped to 101. The result was industry control of what markets were left, with the most destruction happening in energy. What new industries formed mirrored the industrial failure, exacerbating the problem by granting outrageous executive perks and lying to stockholders. The once invincible industrial base was reduced to a mere shadow of its former self.

The unfettered juggernaut was de-clawed.

The financial community was built on exploitation of natural resources, and early on, Wall Street had more power and wealth than Washington. With the move to an agrarian society in an earlier age, money moved out to local communities. The trend was reversed as industry became dominant, and money moved back to Wall Street. By 2008, "The Street" once again had more economic influence than Washington.

With the erosion of the industrial base, banking consolidated its power, creating a few institutions "too big to fail". Congress made politically motivated decisions, encouraging a housing boom with virtually unlimited credit. The financial community exploited this windfall to skim off trillions of community dollars, destroying pensions and security for millions of citizens. The result threw the country into a steep recession; bankruptcy was avoided by the infusion of massive amounts of taxpayer money in a major bailout of the financial community.

It was the financial community's most brazen and outrageous abuse in history, and the nation is not out of the woods; the money and power remain on Wall Street. The legislature has since passed laws to prevent another meltdown, but legislative fixes will not solve the problem. Legislative oversight committees were major culprits in the meltdown in the first place, and a potential future risk will only be resolved by building a stable economic infrastructure.

The transfer of economic power to the financial sector and the transfer of wealth-creating industries overseas have produced drastic technical consequences. The financial sector is siphoning off our bright young men and women who are moving either to Wall Street or to other countries to become immediate millionaires. To many, that's an easy choice compared to going to Detroit to build better and more efficient autos. In 2007, 47% of Harvard graduates went into finance or consulting, a loss for our once unbeatable industrial community.

Possibly more significant is the transfer of wealth and power ever upward, which has created an elitist community with 1% of the population owning 99% of the wealth. This income redistribution is a frightening scenario for citizens living in poverty. It should also be a concern for the wealthy. A nation in which a small portion of the population own most of the wealth, particularly with high levels of poverty, will ultimately result in drastic, disruptive changes. A healthy community requires a proportional balance. As we face the election of 2012, the street demonstrations should not be taken lightly!

Then there are the trade imbalances that are transferring our wealth overseas. Like children with their first credit cards, we have gone into debt, living today with no concern for tomorrow. The Chinese are concerned, because they have a trillion dollars of our IOUs to collect, and they aren't sure we'll be able to pay.

We face concern and anxiety in the 2012 election year regarding how to handle expanded social requirements like healthcare when our economic base is eroding. Joblessness is rampant, working citizens have to cut corners, long-anticipated retirements must be delayed, and poverty continues to grow.

As we face the 2012 election, citizens realize that the wealth created by the unfettered juggernaut has been wasted. A vacuous political system, a vicious financial community, and a fragmented government have reduced the country to near-bankruptcy. Our children and their children will probably never achieve the nation's prior standard of living.

But there is hope!

We still have the greatest technical talent in the world and enough wealth to recover. The economy can be reinvigorated with a new economic infrastructure. To accomplish this, the hodge-podge of laws and rules created by government

must be overhauled. There are hundreds of billions of dollars of waste that can be eliminated if the economy can be
brought under control. There is also an underground economy handling shady market transactions. Given estimates
are in the hundreds of billions of dollars, there is a huge
potential income through elimination of shady business
tactics, tax evasion, fraud and other abuses.

How to tame the beast and save hundreds of billions of dollars will be one of the recommended fixes.

CHAPTER 17

The Socio-Economic System

The combination of a fragmented institutional government and the unfettered juggernaut has created a fragile socio-economic system. The unfettered juggernaut created the most wealth in the history of the world, but institutional failure has brought the country close to bankruptcy. Government never partnered with the economy, and their latest failure was the 2008 meltdown that required a Government bailout.

The unfettered juggernaut has been both a boon and a hazard. In booming times, the country goes on a spending spree, and the economy gets out of balance. By the time we anticipate a slowdown, it is too late to make adjustments, which exacerbates the magnitude of the resulting recession. The 2008 recession was a triple whammy because of this boom and bust phenomenon coupled with erratic Congressional actions and the financial community abuse.

There are some who maintain that there should be an unregulated institutional system similar to the boom time economic system. Their logic is flawed; if the socio-economic and institutional systems are out of sync, severe adjustments are inevitable and a recession is the result. This has been proven time and again.

The current government is unable to achieve socio-economic stability for a number of reasons. The nation does not have a tracking and warning system to identify potential downturns. The Treasury Department has never developed economic models to stabilize the economy. The financial community has never shown any interest in providing economic stabilization, seeming instead to thrive on uncertainty. Congress' political manipulations are more important to them than providing a stable government. Neither government nor private economists have provided any level of direction, having a thousand divergent views. The result is a rambling and uncoordinated institutional effort, adding, among other things, new social services to an economy that cannot pay for them.

So how do we get the economy and the socio-economic systems in sync? The first order of business is to implement a new economic infrastructure fix to provide institutional, economic synergy and to develop a tracking and warning system so the nation knows where it is and where it is going.

CHAPTER 18

Overall Government Recapitulation

In examining what we have said so far, we find a systemic enigma, a dysfunctional institutional process supported by an unfettered economic base. The founders' vision is ignored, and we have a government that was built in back room deals. To try to make any sense of it is fruitless, but we can learn from the failures.

The obvious greatest failure is that of Congress, which was well covered in the institutional review. A branch given the most significant role within the Constitution simply failed, not only in its institutional responsibility but in the shallow demeanor of its members.

The political system is one of the significant failures, though it does point out the inherent weakness of representative government. The election/reelection process is a catch-22 situation that requires potential candidates to pander to local pressures even if they are detrimental to the overall community. It becomes a double edged sword as political payback puts unqualified politicians in positions of great responsibility. The political takeover of Government has created a fragmented infrastructure that has allowed virtually all potential deficiencies to surface.

A major deficiency is the lack of control over the financial community, which has taken over the economy, creating an elitist situation in which 1% of the population owns 99% of the nation's wealth. Whether or not this was by design, it has provided the funding base for a lobbyist community that virtually controls the lawmaking process. Again the recent Supreme Court decision on campaign contributions support this dangerous condition.

Representation, the very essence of the democratic process, has been lost. Presidential elections, the only semblance of representation, are a circus and a farce.

Governmental structure is completely inadequate to the needs of the present and future.

In summary, the current government is saddled with a chaotic mix of rules, regulations, laws, practices and misguided dreams. This is not a good systemic base for a future government.

Given this rather pathetic scenario, let's take a fresh look at the world of today and try to make realistic decisions for the future.

CHAPTER 19

A New Global Benchmark

We have revisited the state of current government, which is not very promising. Before we talk about fixes, we need to establish a benchmark for a new beginning, a position paper on the United States in a new world.

The world of the founders in 1776 was a far cry from today. The British and French Empires, along with the Dutch, controlled much of world trade, and it was primarily exploitive. Open markets were later created and enhanced by the US, which extended its industrial strength to much of the world. Yankee ingenuity and a free and open society with unlimited resources created a powerhouse in international trade, which added to the wealth of the nation.

Today is a new world! These US-enhanced open markets are being filled by emerging nations with capital-intensive governments, governments that are working hand in glove with their economies to minimize costs and maximize industrial production. These nations have lower labor costs, giving them inroads to global markets, including exports to the US.

In addition to increased imports, the US trade imbalance is exacerbated by massive outsourcing. Apple, one of the nation's largest electronic retailers, has virtually all of its manufacturing done in China. One city alone consists of 400.000 jobs that are totally committed to Apple products. This is not to single out Apple as a renegade; virtually all electronics purchased in the US are made by Asian firms. But while the economic conditions caused by this trend are threatening, an even greater concern is the transfer of US technical know-how into foreign hands.

So any strategy to increase income and improve government must address this basic issue. Our labor costs are still much higher than much of the world, even though US labor unions have recently taken significant cuts to ameliorate this condition. It will be years before there is anything approaching parity between US labor costs and those of the global economy.

Another benchmark that must be addressed is finance. The US was probably the greatest factor in creating the global financial world of today, and the US Dollar is the strongest global currency. It is also a bell weather for the global economy. The value of the dollar has been inflated by both internal and global forces, which with our high labor costs constitute a double whammy in the world marketplace. The US financial segment is a ticking time bomb that will wreak havoc if not brought under control. One needs only to look at the current EU crisis as a case in point.

This benchmark emphasizes a systemic truth called balance. When a system is not in balance it fails! This is true of all systems, physical or otherwise. We saw it in government's failure to curb financial excesses. We saw it in government's political behavior (or lack thereof) leading up to the 2008 meltdown. We saw it in banks that had become too big to fail. Now we see it in the government of Greece, which is bankrupt as a result of excessive social programs.

The point is that no one community segment can have enough power to endanger the nation! We came perilously close in the 1980's regarding energy, and we are still not out of the woods. As of this date, the single most dangerous segment of our nation is the financial community, which must be brought under control. This can only be done with a new economic infrastructure.

In summary, we must recognize the frailty of our current government and the need for action in a new global universe. We cannot continue the present practices; if substantial steps are not taken, our nation will soon become just another third world country.

CHAPTER 20

Fix Strategy

We have defined the problems, so how do we fix them?

First, all citizens must acknowledge that the failure is theirs. One can point fingers and talk about others' failures to meet their responsibilities, but in the final analysis, malaise is the culprit. Citizens either ignored their responsibility or turned it over to others, creating a vacuum allowing inadequacies to surface and expand.

So what do we do? There are radicals who would replace the current system, but the only logical answer is to fix it. In spite of Its failures, the Democratic Republic is the best governmental system in the world. The failures in implementation were man-made, but the basic structure is sound. The achievement of the visionaries of the 1700's in selecting a type of government for the people is as valid today as it was at that time.

So how do we fix the existing system? The simple answer is found at the ballot box. The mechanism for fixes has been in place since the inception of our government; it just hasn't been used well.

The current street marches are the first significant evidence of citizen concern with government in a long time. While their concerns are valid, they cannot articulate a platform for rejuvenation. The elitist community is wallowing in wealth while families are living out of their automobiles if they are lucky enough to have one. Castigating the wealthy is useless—wealth comes and goes—because the problem is the system. The Constitutional framework is a viable governmental system, but it has not been used to create the institutional and economic infrastructures needed. Leadership has not been equal to the task and has been dominated by a political process that places ideology over people.

An example is the Tea Party, which threw many legislators out of office in the 1010 election. The movement was to cut governmental spending, which was a viable objective. Its failure was that its singular objective was a fight against tax increases. Rather than espousing a bipartisan effort to improve government, its ideological bias ruptured the conservative party and will undoubtedly have an impact on the 2012 election.

The Tea Party movement identifies a danger that citizens must avoid if government is to be fixed. The effort must be completely bipartisan. Any politically-based effort will fail and will probably create even more erosion.

The starting strategy for "fixes" must be to improve leadership. There is an old saw that essentially says government is bad but my guys are OK. So the same "OK" guys keep getting elected, and nothing ever changes. Teams within each

Congressional District could select the best candidates for office regardless of party. Support those who commit to change government and reestablish the Constitutional vision. Remove those from office who have supported the status quo.

In six years Congress could be cleansed of inadequate leadership through the election process. This probably sounds quite radical, but it is unfortunately essential. I think once leaders get a clear message that changes must be made, they will either support the effort or take the pension and leave.

The situation is too critical to compromise.

I am sure the average citizen does not realize the significance of this threat!

We will now move into specific fixes. We will begin with the economic fix and then move onto the institutional fixes.

CHAPTER 21

The Economic Fix

The economy is a major element in our country, probably the most critical, in our present condition. We might survive a few more years with institutional failure, but a few more years of economic chaos could spell bankruptcy for the nation.

The analysis of the economy and its problems was well documented in Chapter 16. The unfettered juggernaut created the greatest wealth in the world, but it has become a loose cannon through government inadequacy and a exploitative financial community. Wall Street has more power than government, an untenable condition.

This fix is to create a healthy economy, provide jobs for daily living, and allow people to save for investments that will provide a reasonable retirement benefit. There is also a need for financial security, so internal threats such as identify theft must be addressed. The financial system must be brought under control; the nation must have a socioeconomic system that guarantees the integrity and security of both citizens and their money.

The nation must have the most efficient and productive economy to maintain its position in the new world. The problem is not lack of money or technology; in spite of the China bubble we still have more money and better technology than any country in the world. The economic system is a critical mass, and there cannot be a bright future for the nation if it is not brought under control.

A new socio-economic infrastructure would go far beyond the economy itself. It would provide substantial payback and would also address many institutional problems. In a dynamic industrial community, there will always be changes in technology and the inevitable resultant unemployment; but the worst possible reaction is to put out-of-work citizens on the dole. With a cooperative relationship between the economic community and government, potential unemployment can be anticipated and steps taken to minimize the impact.

A new economic infrastructure is a critical need; however, there is another concomitant element we must address, and that is sharing the responsibility. Taxation is anathema to many citizens, but it is a necessary part of the governmental equation. Taxation started as a way to pay for building roads around the estates and communities when the country was forming. It was based on wealth and was called a property tax. As social needs developed, additional monies were needed. Since there was a collection system already in place, new taxes were added to the property tax. Taxing the citizenry soon became the primary method for raising government funds.

Property tax in and of itself has some merit, enforcing definition of legal boundaries, values, and providing a base for zoning. But it is destructive when senior citizens lose their homes because they cannot pay property taxes that have been inflated by other needs. The crux of the issue is that taxation is a necessary element, but the nation's hodgepodge of systems does not provide for equal sharing. With a new economic infrastructure, we could better manage the money flow, identify potential new sources for sharing, and close the loopholes in the current process.

In summation, a new socio-economic system is a necessity to address the myriad economic and institutional needs of the community. Stability is critical, and this can only be established with an integrated relationship between the economy and government.

The new economic infrastructure will require a new department and staff. A topnotch team of economists, statisticians and professional managers will be necessary. It is difficult to recommend additional staff in our current economic plight; however, many would be recruited from current staff.

The potential gains will be multiples of the costs involved. Gains will be in both savings, as more effective practices are developed, and in revenues, as a more productive country sells its products around the world. The governments of other nations, such as China, Korea and Brazil, have established integrated government/economic relationships to enhance their international sales. The United States must meet this challenge.

So how do we create this new economic infrastructure? It can be accomplished with a federal computer/communication network. Establishing a network to process and monitor all community financial transactions is not a major change; it would be accomplished through the consolidation of already existing systems into a new, singular system. For example, the credit card system has probably already covered the major portion of transactions. The problem is that current financial systems have no overall control.

A new singular system would guarantee the integrity of all economic/financial transactions. A daily balancing of the community books would provide explicit detail of the financial state-of-the-state. Every financial transaction within the community would be processed through a single network. This may sound improbable to citizens who still think of the computer as a black hole, but it would actually be much easier than the institutional fixes we face.

To allay the fears of those concerned with technical innovation, the processing time would be a fraction of the time used in the present disaggregated system. Elimination of redundancy and duplication could reduce the volumes to perhaps a fifth of those we have today.

Security is of course the major concern, and the best technical resources in the world would be involved in the development of the new system. Hacking would have to be a federal offense with long-term criminal penalties. Security would be paramount, and both personal and business funds would be guaranteed.

The new system would make the market completely dynamic, with no constraints whatever; all business transactions would be processed and reported immediately, with no waiting weeks or months to know the state-of-the-state.

This is a long-term fix. A properly designed system would provide the necessary monitoring of and for our economy forever. It is an essential requirement today and a critical requirement for the future; no country will survive economically in the future without this capability.

The initial phase would be the creation of a user database and establishing allowable transaction types. The user database would identify all legal entities of the nation, and only legitimate transaction types would be processed, thereby eliminating underground activity. This phase would capture the money flow and guarantee that the system is in balance.

The next phase would open the system to both government and private functions. Major governmental functions such as IRS, Social Security, Welfare, etc. could be supported, as the integrity and security of personal information will already have been provided for. The ultimate objective is consolidating the entire community/governmental/ financial universe into one stream, with a complete guarantee of the integrity thereof.

When fully operational the new system would provide substantial enhancements.

A long-term suggestion for taxation is implementation of a "flat" income tax; estimates of increased revenues are in the hundreds of billions of dollars. A flat tax could be implemented easily and quickly, once the new infrastructure was in place.

Another long-term financial objective is currency reform. New currency could be issued and the old phased out. In the new system, the use of currency would be strongly curtailed. This would be the final step in eliminating currency now used to support unhealthy business practices.

The benefits of this new system are mind-boggling. There is probably some redundancy in the list below, for which I ask the reader's indulgence. I'm equally sure that the list is incomplete; there will be benefits beyond those listed.

The benefits of eliminating redundancy and duplication, plus improved audit capabilities, are quite obvious. The more significant benefit would be the ability to define in more detail the logic involved in the financial transactions being processed.

Economists would have a completely new dimension in understanding the details of our socio-economic system. New and more precise decisions could be made for the benefit of both government and the private sector. Economists and government planners would have a real life model to use for the analysis required to maintain a stable government.

There have been no economists in history who have had this ability. This would eliminate political smokescreen and provide a realistic economic base with a state-of-the-state report that every citizen could understand.

While the value to the economists and government planners is more than adequate justification for developing a new economic infrastructure, there are an infinite number of additional tangible benefits that can provide significant payback.

Accurate and timely transaction tracking could uncover all kinds of fraud, and abuses in healthcare, welfare, and income tax, among others.

Implementation of a flat income tax could provide hundreds of billions of dollars in increased revenues and lowered administrative costs.

The new system would provide a tracking and warning system, updating government and private citizens alike on current status as well as future trends.

It would provide tremendous efficiency gains through the elimination of paperwork. Personal checks would be supported for a time but eventually eliminated, and transactions would be entered via electronic devices.

It would provide a complete restructuring of the federal money flow, the treasury, and banking; all financial services would be integrated into a single audit-proof process.

When fully operational, social services (Social Security, Welfare, Healthcare, etc.) would be integrated into the money flow and work from a common base. The savings from decreased bureaucratic fumbling would be astronomical. There is virtually no limit to the efficiency and synergy gains in governmental operations.

Currency reform could bring out billions of dollars buried in the old infrastructure, and it could recover unknown value through the elimination of the various kinds of fraud mentioned above.

In summary, the new infrastructure would provide hundreds of billions of dollars to the economy through efficiency gains, increased revenues, and more effective management of the economic system. It would eliminate financial constraints and open the door to a renewed and vigorous economy.

Perhaps most important, the nation could finally get its finances out of the hands of Wall Street, after two centuries of imbalance.

This only scratches the surface of the potential benefits; the list is limited only by the reader's imagination.

But there would be more enhancements:

The new user database could, with minor expansion, include all citizens, thereby replacing the current Census Bureau database. The 2010 census cost was over a billion dollars and will provide only a limited level of precision. By

2020 a new online system could save billions of dollars and provide a level of accuracy not possible today. This would also improve the inaccurate citizen representation caused by the current manual census taking efforts.

It could also be the basis for a federal security system. Instant personal identification is needed today and will be an even more critical for the future. Identity theft is a current and future problem, and terrorism is not going to go away. A citizen database linking an individual through a computer network could provide immediate ID. We could throw away the stacks of identity cards that stuff our wallets and purses, and we could board airplanes without being patted down.

I have tried to estimate some ball park figures as to the actual cost benefits from the new system. Though that is a highly speculative activity, the only figures I can come up with are in the hundreds of billions if not trillions of dollars. I leave it up to readers to make their own estimates.

There is no way our country can regain its strength without a stable economic infrastructure and the degree of accountability and stability it would provide. Given our open community, we could improve the free market system and provide the transparency so lacking in the past. The community would finally know the real state-of-the-state.

I have two final comments on this subject:

The establishments, particularly the financial ones, will bash this fix as more government intrusion into business. That is not the intent. The intent is to develop synergy between government and the economic community, to create additional wealth and stabilize the economy.

For those readers who are not comfortable with this recommendation I would add a final thought. *This fix is going to happen.* It is a future requirement that no government will be able to do without.

There are choices about how to do it. It can be done professionally at minimum costs today with significant benefits, or it can develop empirically, through normal bureaucratic fumbling. It can be implemented professionally and be fully operational in ten years, or it can develop empirically in twenty five to fifty years. If it is *not* done immediately, the additional costs will be in the trillions of dollars and could well make the difference between solvency and bankruptcy.

CHAPTER 22

A Note of Caution

Whatever fixes are selected will take years or even decades to implement. Before we tackle institutional fixes, we need to take a brief look ahead and anticipate world changes and their implications to a fix strategy. I don't think anyone would question that this century will see the most changes ever in the history of civilization. We are already seeing the world financial crisis, Arab Spring, the threatened Euro, emerging nations, and world energy issues; the list is endless.

The US is in the best position to cope with the changing world. We have the greatest strength, a homogenous population with a single language, and an ability to communicate across the complete spectrum. Changes must be made, but they must be managed with great care; the government is too fragile for violent change.

Before the end of the century, I am sure systemic requirements will have an impact on government structure and organization. Long-term strategy should anticipate these changing needs and work toward meeting them; however, radical structural changes for short term benefit should be avoided. There are many short-term fixes that can provide significant benefit without major disruption. The fixes being recommended are not radical or revolutionary; they are practical solutions intended mostly to address short-comings in implementing the Constitutional vision.

I understand the frustration of the street marchers, but I also believe I understand the steps that must be taken to get our nation back on track. It will take time to make adjustments, and their frustrations will not go away quickly; but a steady, practical approach is the only way to go.

CHAPTER 23
The Legislative Fix

Major legislative shortcomings were well defined in Chapter 8. Their failure in fulfilling the role assigned to the Congress by the Constitution has allowed the development of a fragile government that is failing in its responsibilities to the nation. A strong Congress should have fulfilled its Constitutional role, but since their default, the course of history was irrecoverably changed. Citizens must address this problem and determine the appropriate solutions; continuation of the present Congressional practices will only lead to further erosion of a fragmented government.

Congress is made up of citizen representatives of the people, and that interface cannot be totally disrupted. The institutional government is too fragile to sustain a major disruption. The recommended fixes will be to repair the damage done by the original default and to allow Congress to achieve the original constitutional objectives. Following is a strategy, including some short-term fixes that can turn the ailing system around and prepare for the future.

As far as I can determine, most of the fixes are within institutional authority and should not require Constitutional changes. The problem will be making Congress get off the dime and start working. Political ideology is not going to fix the problem; it has been one of the greatest deterrents to effective problem-solving. Citizens must accept the very difficult managerial role that has become quite popular on TV; they must learn to say "you're fired". Until Congress gets their act together, the criteria for election should be a commitment to necessary change, not to political dogma.

First and foremost is the limitation of political intransigence. We should reorganize the chambers by State, with leadership roles equitably shared. Congress is not a sports arena, it is the institutional foundation of government. Lawmaking is not a game of win or lose; there are no winners, and the only losers are citizens abused by inadequate leadership.

We should rewrite legislative procedures with complete transparency and put them online for citizens to review. Some necessary executive sessions could be accepted, but their purposes should be identified and reasonable periods established by which time they must be made public.

Term limits should be initiated, both for holding office and for serving as committee chairs.

Financial responsibility must be established; the political motivations leading to the 2008 meltdown should never be repeated.

The Legislature should work with the Judiciary to develop a more precise legal language and to actively begin a cleanup of the nation's laws.

We should stagger elections, scheduling Congressional elections as far as possible from Presidential elections to minimize the disturbances caused by major election shifts.

We should eliminate the lobbyist community and the danger it represents to the nation.

I think this is an adequate beginning for Legislative Fixes, though there will be additional corollary recommendations with other fixes that follow.

CHAPTER 24

The Executive Fix

The evolution of the Presidency into a pseudo-monarchial entity has exacerbated the governmental erosion of the past 50 years. Just as it needs the Legislature, the nation needs a Chief Executive and will as long as government exists. So how do we control the Presidency for the present and provide a logical development path for a future more balanced government?

Most of the problem lies with the political process that has made presidential elections a Barnum and Bailey circus. For young readers, P. T. Barnum was an early showman and scam artist known for his comment, "There is a sucker born every minute." There seems to be no orchestrated or organized political effort to provide qualified nominees. Candidates just seem to come out of the woodwork every four years; this will be discussed further under the Political Fix. In the meantime, there is a change that should help.

First, we should consider the electoral process itself. Various methods for representation have been tried throughout history, and to date there is no best solution. The weakness of the current process has allowed a takeover by the political establishment; winning is only a matter of deep pockets and carrying a few swing states.

We need to broaden the electoral base for better representation. I recommend that we use the 435 congressional districts as the base; the winner would be the one who garners the most districts. If there are multiple candidates, the unlikely chance of a tie would have to be addressed..

This would change political strategy completely. It would require political parties to target 435 districts rather than the 10 or 12 states they now address. Local districts that have been disenfranchised in the past would become dynamic fighters in the selection process. This should provide candidates from a broader base.

Next, we should minimize the disturbances involved in every change in office. I recommend a seven-year single term for the President, with Congressional elections staggered in the off years. A seven-year term would allow an effective leader to achieve his stated objectives and would hopefully minimize his political baggage while in office..

We should increase the President's salary to attract qualified candidates, perhaps to ten million dollars a year plus expenses, with a substantial life time pension.

The political implications regarding the Executive Branch have also been reviewed under Political Fixes, and executive responsibility was also addressed in the section on Governmental Structure and Organization.

In 2012, we should choose a Chief Executive who will refuse to accept the status quo, accept the reality that the government is ineffective, and lead the effort to institute realistic fixes.

Chapter 25

The Judiciary Fix

Judiciary shortcomings were covered in Chapter 8. The only possible conclusion is that the judiciary, though given the most honorable place in government by the Constitution, has failed to meet its responsibilities in every way, from the courts to tort reform to standards of conduct.

This is an area in which the legal community must cleanse itself. This will require a complete change of mindset.

The legal community is probably the most ingrained profession in existence. I have worked with various technical societies, and after a reasonable assimilation time I have usually been able to establish a dialogue. This is just not possible with the legal community. The primary objective of writing laws or contracts is to leave loopholes that can be used later to obviate explicit closure. To achieve even implicit closure is seldom achieved.

Because of my IT background, I would recommend replacing "legalese" with Boolean logic, which would provide a high level of precision. It would certainly be better than the "whereof's" and "wherefor's" that have dominated our institutional systems since their inception.

My rough estimates indicate that the annual costs to the nation for the legal community approach a trillion dollars, or about $5,000 per family. That is approximately what the 2011 Super Committee is trying to save in the next ten years.

CHAPTER 26

The Citizen Fix

This is easy!

Citizens must throw off their malaise and become active participants in government. The nation cannot survive with the current low level of citizen participation. The inability of the street marchers to answer the most basic questions about government was appalling. The nation is burdened with governmental inadequacy, but it cannot survive with the current level of citizen support.

Finally, there is one frightening movement that could bring down the democratic republic; many government leaders have signed a contract to refuse any effort to raise taxes. They have done this under threat of massive funding for their opponent in their next election.

I cannot conceive of this ethical breach of responsibility or citizen default. I assume that the perpetrators of this heinous effort have researched the legality and feel they are not in jeopardy. However, it certainly seems in conflict with that part of the oath of both the House and the Senate that reads, "…I will well and faithfully discharge the duties of the office on which I am about to enter…"

If this effort is allowed to continue, it could lead to a "shadow" monarchy, by which a single individual or power group could completely control the nation. This is exactly the thing Constitutional visionaries tried to avoid. It is contrary to the constitutional intent for a balance of power, and it is possibly more threatening than an actual monarchy. No leader who has ever signed or supported this contract should ever be allowed to hold public office.

If it is constitutionally legal, Congress should immediately pass a law countering this threat to the nation. If necessary, a Constitutional amendment should be initiated.

I am sure the average citizen does not realize the significance of this threat!

It would be very shallow of me to expect every reader to agree with everything I have covered. But citizens should not walk away from the problem and do nothing. There are other information sources than this book, and voters should seek them out. Make no mistake: continued citizen malaise will spell the end of this great nation as we know it.

CHAPTER 27
The Political Fix

The problem is *not* the two-party system. Liberals and conservatives provide a balance and have been a stabilizing factor in partially offsetting our fragile and ineffective government. The proof is that we haven't yet tripped over the line into monarchy or socialism.

So why are we in such a trauma over the political process?

There are two critical failures of this process. First, they have not met their primary obligation of providing quality governmental leadership; second, the parties have so infiltrated government that decision-making is constrained by party dogma. The country is managed by the political process rather than by the will of the people.

This is a ridiculous scenario for the nation. Neither party has the confidence of the people, and both, through their abysmal party leadership, have become a joke. The smokescreen and hysteria that each espouse have contributed to their limited stature.

The primary responsibility of the political process is the development of adequate government leadership. Liberals and conservatives provide a critical balance in government and have much to contribute. But if they are to be effective, they must articulate their precise doctrines and enforce them within their membership. They must provide clear and consistent requirements for qualified government leadership. Carnival methods for capturing the next election must be stopped.

Most critical is the double-edged sword of political involvement in the inner workings of government; that must be stopped. Staffing of government positions with election supporters produces ineffective government and creates major disturbances that resonate across the entire governmental and community spectrum.

It is incongruous to me that neither party recognizes its vacuity or the inadequacy of their governing. Dedicated conservatives and liberals have much to contribute to a balanced government. If they do not clean up their act, defining and articulating their objectives, they will be replaced by new parties and relegated to the radical fringe elements at the edges of the community spectrum.

Acceptance by the political establishment of the above viewpoints would go a long way toward establishing trust in their parties.

Chapter 28

Final Recapitulation

Before we talk about implementation strategy, let's take a quick look at what we've found so far.

The Constitutional framework for the new government gave all lawmaking responsibility to Congress. Congress not only failed in lawmaking, but it allowed itself to be dominated by a political process that places ideology before the best interests of the nation. Congressional failure has allowed the legal and judiciary communities to dominate all aspects of government since the beginning.

The transfer of power to the Executive Branch has created a pseudo-monarchy, allowing the political process to dominate not only Congress but the actual running of government. Presidential elections have taken on the role of a political placebo, creating a constant string of disturbances to the economy.

The infiltration of the political community into government has created a fragile governmental infrastructure. The wealth-creating economy has never been integrated into or coordinated with the institutional government.

The financial community has exploited an ineffective government, siphoning money off to an elitist community that dominates government through personal and lobbyist funding.

The nation, bound up by a hodge-podge of laws and rules, is completely out of control. This can only be fixed with enlightened leadership and a dynamic citizenry.

Citizens must accept the fact that their country is in grave danger.

I am sure that every citizen is concerned with the current state-of-the-state today. There are major issues, including energy needs, a no-win war, healthcare, and a myriad of other concerns. But citizens must also realize that we have critical governmental issues that will erode the nation further. If not fixed, the systemic flaws that have been pointed out in this book will continue to erode our governmental process and threaten the wellbeing of our children for generations to come.

I would like to point out a personal experience from WWII. A German airplane was circling overhead trying to get a fix on us. He missed us, hitting the battalion behind us and causing several casualties. About the same time, news came in over the field phones of the death of President Roosevelt.

I clearly remember the sinking sensation that I felt. FDR was a hero who had led the nation out of the depression and turned it around. I was under fire in a slit trench in the middle of a war, and I had a baby daughter whom I had never seen. I remember the feeling of dread that came over me at that time, not just for myself, but for the future of our country.

The feeling of dread I have for my country right now is greater than what I felt then. We have a country that is eroding faster than France and England did during their collapse as world leaders. Every facet of our government and economy is in trouble, and we do not have the leadership to turn things around.

Concerned citizens must rise to meet this need, starting at the local level, through dialogs with neighbors and friends. We need to roll up our sleeves and start making the fixes we've been discussing.

A new economic infrastructure fix could be started quickly. It is not dependent on institutional fixes, and it is one of the most significant fixes given current conditions. It is the only hope for financial stability, and for today's workers it is the only guarantee of a secure retirement.

Be assured, it will be fought tooth and nail by the financial community; but it must be done. Wall Street's hold on government must be broken. An excellent start would be a dynamic 2012 presidential candidate who supports a new economy as a major platform plank.

A constitutional amendment would be required to restructure the election schedule and change or modify term limits. This can't be done by 2012, but it could be by 2016 with adequate motivation. I suspect three or four more election fiascos will bring the entire institutional base crashing down. The disturbances they create are just too great for government stability.

Changes to legislative procedures are completely within Congress' constitutional powers and could begin immediately.

I don't know the degree of authority the Executive Branch has over governmental structure, but some improvement to the current flat organization could be begin immediately. Again, this could be a significant 2012 platform plank.

We must be realistic in our expectations, but we must also be determined to make the necessary changes to get this great nation back on track. My greatest concern is continuing citizen malaise, which would allow the political system to expand the smokescreen and hysteria, convincing people there is no problem. That would be a disaster.

The effort must be completely bipartisan. Supporters of all parties should be able to have a dialogue with others in establishing a stable government that will meet the needs of all. A government driven by ingrained ideology cannot be effective, as has been proven beyond all doubt by present and past administrations.

We are embarking on a new venture. My hope is for the commitment of a major portion of citizens to make the necessary decisions in leadership selection. Leadership is essential in a representative democracy, and it has been usurped by an inept political system. *The people must take it back.*

I hope we can achieve fixes through use of the internet and the new social media; they offer opportunities never before conceived. I think a low profile is the way to go. Street marches and banners open the door to all sorts of unwelcome diversions.

If Egypt can be freed using Twitter, we can certainly initiate a dialogue among our fellow citizens.

I would like to think that a good start might be to loan or buy a friend a copy of this book. It is an inexpensive gift that I hope will provide a starting point for a community dialogue. It is available on e-books at a very low price, and Amazon Kindle users can download it free for 30 days.

I have established a web-site, USGOVFIX.COM that will start as a bulletin board to assist in a community dialogue.

Thank you for reading this; now let's get to work.

www.ingramcontent.com/pod-product-compliance
Lightning Source LLC
Chambersburg PA
CBHW062035280526
45788CB00003B/1012